Bikes and Boards

Lisa Greathouse

Bikes and Boards

Publishing Credits

Editorial Director
Dona Herweck Rice

Associate Editors
James Anderson
Torrey Maloof

Editor-in-Chief
Sharon Coan, M.S.Ed.

Creative Director
Lee Aucoin

Illustration Manager
Timothy J. Bradley

Publisher
Rachelle Cracchiolo, M.S.Ed.

Science Consultant
Scot Oschman, Ph.D.

Teacher Created Materials
5301 Oceanus Drive
Huntington Beach, CA 92649-1030
http://www.tcmpub.com

ISBN 978-1-4333-0303-6

Printed by: 590835
Printed in: China

Table of Contents

The Science of Bikes and Boards

When you climb on your bike or kick off on a skateboard, you might not think about how they work. You just take off and go! But there's a lot of science that goes into the world of bikes and skateboards. And when you see a snowboarder speed down a slope or a surfer "hangin' ten," that is science at work, too!

There are many athletes who ride bikes and boards for more than fun. Some perform thrilling stunts and reach record-breaking speeds. They call it "extreme sports." These athletes look for the biggest wave or the steepest slope. For them, it is all about taking risks. But it is also about stretching the limits of **physics** (FIZ-iks). Physics is the study of force and motion.

These boarders are getting some "big air."

Some bicycle riders can perform amazing, gravity-defying tricks. Luckily, this rider remembered to wear his "brain bucket."

What's THAT Mean?

It seems that every sport has its own language. Some words have meanings that are easy to figure out. Others do not seem to make any sense at all!

Sport	Slang Word and Meaning
Cycling	brain bucket = helmet gravity check = fall
Skateboarding	deck = the wooden plank of the skateboard bail = to jump off your skateboard to avoid a crash
Surfing	hangin' ten = surfing with 10 toes over the nose of the board ankle biter = small wave
Snowboarding/ Skateboarding	halfpipe = U-shaped ramp big air = a big jump

Get Pedaling!

Do you remember learning how to ride a bike? It may have taken you a few tries before you got the hang of it. When you are learning, the tricky part is keeping the bike from falling over. That is because a bike stays up only when it is in **motion** (unless it is leaning against something). Motion is how, where, and why something moves.

Motion is a big part of sports. Without motion, a skateboarder would never land a jump. A snowboarder would never get down the hill. And a **cyclist** would never get anywhere!

Bicycles Through History

1817

The Walking Machine

You used your feet to walk this wooden machine along.

1865

The Bone Shaker

Pedals were added to the front wheel of this wooden machine.

1870

The High Wheel Bicycle

The front wheel was made larger so the rider could get farther with one turn of the wheel.

1886

The Rover

This bike had the basic features of today's bicycles. Everyone wanted one!

But nothing moves by itself. For there to be motion, there needs to be a **force**. A force is a push or a pull that causes movement. When you are riding a bike, the force of your muscles makes the pedals move. That force is the "engine" of your bike.

Training wheels can help you balance your bike until you learn to keep it in motion.

1930

The Cruiser

The wide tires of this bike made it popular for riding on the beach.

1970s

The Racing Bike

Low handlebars and skinny tires were popular in the 1970s and 1980s.

1980s

The Mountain Bike

This heavier bike with wider tires became popular in the 1980s and 1990s.

2000s

The Hybrid Bike

This is a mix of mountain and racing bikes.

Defy Gravity on Your Bike!

If you do not get your bike moving in a forward motion, what is it that makes it fall over? **Gravity** (GRAV-uh-tee). Gravity is the force that holds us on the ground and keeps us from floating into space. The **rotation** of the wheels acts as an anti-gravity force. So when you ride your bike, you are defying gravity!

There is a type of math named after Isaac Newton. It is called Newtonian Mechanics.

Newton's Laws of Motion

There are laws to help us understand why and how things move. We have the work of scientist Isaac Newton to thank for these laws. Newton lived in the 1600s. His first law says that an object will keep doing what it is doing unless an outside force acts on it. So if an object is not moving it will stay where it is. But a moving object will keep moving in the same direction forever. That is, unless something gets in its way.

Newton's second law says that when a force acts on an object, the object will speed up or slow down. It also says that the more **mass** an object has, the more force you need to move it. That's why a full shopping cart is harder to push than an empty one.

The third law says that for every action, there is an equal and opposite reaction. That means that whenever an object pushes another object, it gets pushed back just as hard. For example, the wheels of a bike grip the road as they spin and try to push the road backwards. The immoveable road pushes the wheels forward with equal force.

How Do Your Brakes Work?

Just as important as moving on a bicycle is stopping! The brakes on a bike use **friction** (FRIK-shuhn) to slow you down. Friction is a force that happens whenever things rub against each other. When you squeeze the handbrakes on a bike, force is applied to the tire. This causes pads to rub against the metal rim that holds the tire. The more **pressure** on the rim, the slower the wheel can turn. That's why you press the handbrakes harder if you need to stop fast!

A Bike for Every Kind of Rider

When you think about it, a bicycle is a pretty amazing machine. Riding it is a great way to get from one place to another. It is good exercise. You can race it on tracks, roads, and through mountains. Some people even do stunts on their bikes. And a bike does not need any extra fuel—the person riding provides all the energy it needs. The harder you pedal, the faster you go!

There is a bike for every use. Mountain bikes have wide tires. That allows them to grip dirt trails. Racing bicycles are made from lightweight metals. That is because it is easier to move something with less mass. BMX bikes are strong, small, and lightweight. They have knobby tires. That makes them perfect for jumping and racing, even in dirt. Many stunt and racing bikes do not even have brakes!

A Billion!

There are about one billion bicycles in the world. That is twice as many as cars!

BMX

If you have ever seen cyclists performing jumps and other tricks on their bikes, they are probably BMX cyclists. BMX stands for bicycle motocross. BMX racing is done off-road on dirt tracks. Freestyle BMX riders use ramps to perform exciting stunts. These types of bikes have smaller wheels so they can move easily in small places like skate parks.

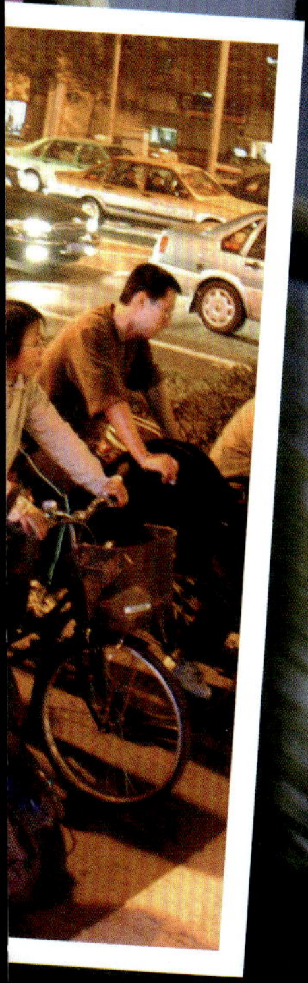

BMX riders can do difficult stunts off dirt jumps.

Testing the Limits

When you think about it, a skateboard is really just a plank of wood on roller-skate wheels. That is hard to believe when you see a skateboarder fly off a high ledge onto a narrow metal handrail! Skateboarders seem to test the limits. They do flips, slides, and turns at top speeds. You might wonder: How do they do that? There is a lot of science behind those tricks.

A good example is the "ollie." It is one of the most popular skateboard tricks. The ollie is a jump that looks like the skater has the board attached to his or her shoes. The skateboarder starts by putting one foot in the center of the board and the other foot on the back end or tail. Then the skater bends his or her knees and drops into a low crouch. The skater slams down on the back of the board. As the board bounces up, the skater jumps. From there, it helps to know a little something about friction and gravity. The friction between the skater's foot and the board drags the board higher. Then gravity takes hold. The board and skater land flat on the ground. It looks like the board never left the skater's shoes!

The "handplant" is another trick used by skaters. Mimi Knoop, a famous skateboarder, does a handplant at a skateboarding event in California.

Who's Ollie?

The "ollie" was invented by Alan "Ollie" Gelfand. Growing up in Florida in the 1970s, Gelfand was a champion skateboarder. Gelfand's friends nicknamed his "no-hands aerial" stunt an ollie. The name stuck. It has become such a basic skateboarding move that ollie has even made it into the dictionary!

No matter what age you are, skateboarding can be good exercise.

deck art

A Place to Call Their Own

Years ago, skateboarders would just skate on the streets in their neighborhoods. But many cities now have their own skate parks. These are cement parks that have built-in ramps and handrails just for skateboarders. You can see some great tricks and thrilling stunts there. Of course, safety is the most important thing when you are skateboarding. Helmets, as well as knee, wrist, and elbow pads, can prevent serious injuries.

The Changing Deck

Skateboards have come a long way in the last 50 years. But the basics have not changed much. A board still has just three parts: the board or deck, the wheels, and the trucks. The trucks connect the wheels to the board. Boards are still made from wood. But the design has changed a lot.

Today's boards curve up at the edges, nose, and tail. This makes the board stronger. It also gives the rider more control to do tricks. New types of wheels allow for more **traction** (TRAK-shun), speed, and smoothness. And some of today's decks really are works of art!

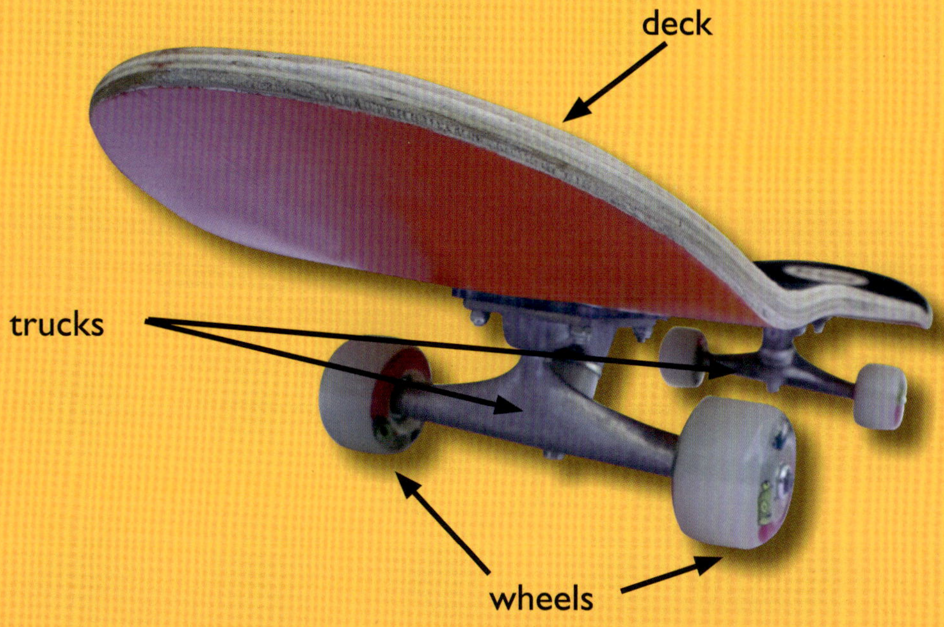

Surfers must have good timing and pay attention to force and gravity to avoid "wiping out."

Waiting for the Wave

Imagine being on a skateboard speeding down a hill. Now imagine that the hill is moving along with you! That is the feeling of riding a wave on a surfboard. The downward pull of gravity is the only force moving you along the watery hill.

Surfers need to have a feel for the ocean and a good eye for waves. They take their boards out into the water and wait for the "perfect" wave. They paddle hard to try to match the speed of the wave. Once the wave starts to carry the board, the surfer jumps to his or her feet. The rushing water propels the surfer to the water's speed. Then gravity takes over, pulling the surfer along the wave. Now the surfer is "riding" the wave. The surfer tries to stay just ahead of the breaking part, or white water, of the wave. If the surfer's toes are just off the edge of the board, then the surfer is "hangin' ten!"

Comeback Kid

Bethany Hamilton started surfing when she was just a toddler. It was not long before she was winning surfing contests in Hawaii. But when she was 13, Bethany was attacked by a 14-foot tiger shark. She lost her arm in the attack. Only a few months later, Bethany was back on her surfboard. Today, she is again winning surfing contests. She inspires others never to give up.

The surfer is tube riding, or "shooting the curl."

Surfing Secrets

Have you ever wondered how a surfer manages to stay on the board? The key to surfing is to be able to shift your **center of mass**, or your balance point, as the wave pulls you along. You want to slide downhill at the same speed the wave moves up under you. If you slide down too fast, you will reach the bottom of the wave too quickly. Too slow, and the wave will outrun you and you will wipe out. The longer the ride, the better!

As in other sports, surfers seem to be taking their sport to the next level. It is becoming more common to see surfers performing tricks out in the ocean. One is called "tube riding." That is when a surfer gets into a position where the wave curls over him or her. The surfer rides in the hollow part of the wave.

Surf Culture

For many people, surfing is not just a sport. It is a way of life. The surfing craze started in Southern California in the 1950s. Since then, surfing has become a part of popular culture. Musical groups write songs about surfing. People who have never been on a surfboard wear "surfer" clothing, like board shorts. There are books and movies about surfing. Even the first skateboards were built to look like small surfboards!

Add Snow and Go!

Take a little skateboarding, a little surfing—add some snow—and you have snowboarding! A snowboard is bigger than a skateboard. But it is smaller than a surfboard.

Snowboarders attach both feet to the board with **bindings**. Unlike skiers, they do not use poles. They use their bodies to steer them as they speed, or shred, down the slope. Some snowboarders seem to defy gravity with their jumps, turns, and mid-air twists. Snowboarding is one of the most popular sports today. It is even an Olympic event!

Gravity is a major force in snowboarding. It keeps the snowboard on the mountain. Gravity also helps the snowboarder gain speed down the slope. The steeper the mountain, the faster the snowboarder goes. That change in speed is called **acceleration** (ak-sel-uh-RAY-shuhn).

Friction helps the snowboarder control the board. Ice and snow are slick, so snowboards just slide. Snowboarders wax the bottom of their boards to make them even more slippery. That cuts down on friction and keeps them moving at top speeds.

The Snurfer?

The first snowboard was called the "Snurfer" (a mix of *snow* and *surfer*). A Michigan man designed it for his daughter in 1965. It was basically a sled that you could stand on. He put two skis together and included a place to put her feet. It was not long before all her friends wanted one, too!

Carving a Turn

It might seem like snowboarders are always leaning one way or another as they whoosh down snowy mountain slopes. That is how they steer. Like surfers, snowboarders must shift their centers of mass to "carve." Carving is leaning into a turn so the snowboard glides downhill on one edge. It is like a knife blade carving the snow. There is less friction, since only the edge of the board is in contact with the snow.

When snowboarders want to stop, they need to act fast! It is tough to keep your balance if you slow down before you stop. Instead, you will see snowboarders making sharp, sideways turns and grinding into the snow when they want to stop. As the snowboarder pushes into the snow, the snow pushes back with equal force. The **collision** between the snowboard and the snow brings the snowboarder to a fast stop.

Wakeboarding

Wakeboarding is a mixture of surfing, snowboarding, and waterskiing. Both of your feet are attached with bindings to a small surfboard. Your board is pulled across the water by a rope attached to a motorboat. Wakeboarding has not been around long. But it is becoming one of the fastest-growing water sports in the world!

Working with the Wind

Whether you are riding a bike or a board, one of the best parts is feeling the wind in your hair. But air movement also slows you down. There are things that athletes do to help them keep their speed—even against the wind.

Some athletes wear clothing that will not slow them down. They wear special speed suits with skin-tight, slippery material. That improves the athlete's **aerodynamics** (air-oh-dye-NAM-iks). That is the way the air flows around a moving object.

An athlete's position can also make a difference. A cyclist who sits straight up in his or her seat will not go as fast as one who crouches low over the handlebars. That is because the air does not hit as many parts of the body.

Lance Armstrong

One of the most famous cyclists of all time is Lance Armstrong. He beat about 200 other cyclists to win the Tour de France a record seven times. The yearly three-week bike race across France covers 3,219 kilometers (2,000 miles)! During his career, Armstrong fought cancer, but kept training—and winning.

personal transporter

electric scooter

electric skateboard

electric bicycle

The Future of Bikes and Boards

We might not know what the bikes and boards of the future will look like. But one thing is for sure: They will be designed for speed. Skateboards, snowboards, and surfboards will give even smoother rides. Their designs will help them react better to the rider's movements. Some boards may have built-in computer chips! They would be able to give riders tips for learning or doing tricks. Better safety gear will reduce injuries.

There are many people who think bicycles are the future of transportation. In fact, some people think they can help solve the world's problems. They cut down on pollution. They save money. They conserve energy. They reduce traffic jams. They are great exercise. In some cities, most people use bikes instead of cars. Will we be riding electric bikes one day? Some people even think that in the future, adults will be riding bikes with three wheels. That's right—tricycles!

High-Tech Handlebars

Bicycle handlebars are not just for steering anymore. Some bikes have on-board computers. They can measure speed, how far you have gone, temperature, and even your heart rate!

Lab: Downhill Racing

Snowboarders wax the bottom of their boards to cut down on friction and help them build up speed. What else would make a snowboard or skateboard change speed?

Materials

- piece of stiff cardboard, at least 45 cm x 30 cm (18 inches x 12 inches)
- blocks or books
- five smooth strips of aluminium foil or waxed paper, each 30 cm x 5 cm (12 inches x 2 inches)
- tape
- small fan
- 120 mL ($\frac{1}{2}$ cup) water
- 15 mL (1 tbsp) butter
- 15 mL (1 tbsp) cornstarch
- salt
- carpenter's square for measuring angle of slope
- checkers
- flag or whistle

Procedure:

1. Tape a short side of each strip of foil or waxed paper to the top edge of the cardboard. Place the strips a minimum of 5 centimeters (2 inches) apart.
2. On the first strip, sprinkle water. On strip two, sprinkle water and salt. On strip three, spread cornstarch. On strip four, spread a thin coat of butter. Position the fan to blow on strip five.

3. Prop the cardboard at a 45-degree angle on books or blocks, creating a slope. Tape the other end of the cardboard to the floor to stabilize it.

4. Divide the class into five teams. Give each team a checker and assign each team a strip. Wave a flag or blow a whistle to have each team release its checker down its strip at the same time.

5. Watch to see which checker reaches the bottom first. Record the sequence, first to last, on a chart like the one below.

6. Have students experiment with different slope angles and compare their findings. Does the angle affect the sequence?

Strip sequence	45–degree slope
First place	Strip #_____
Second place	Strip #_____
Third place	Strip #_____
Fourth place	Strip #_____
Fifth place	Strip #_____

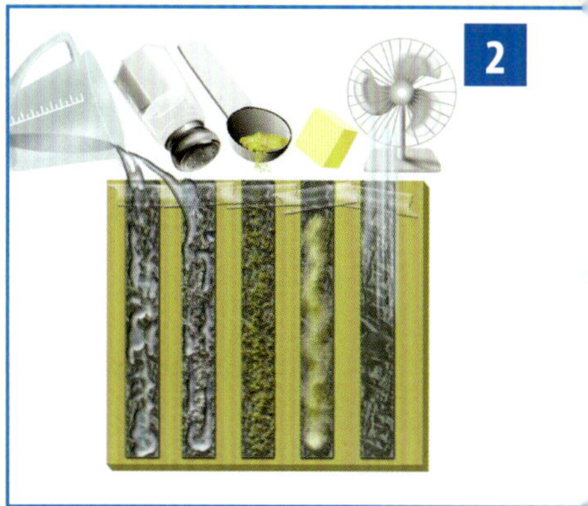

2

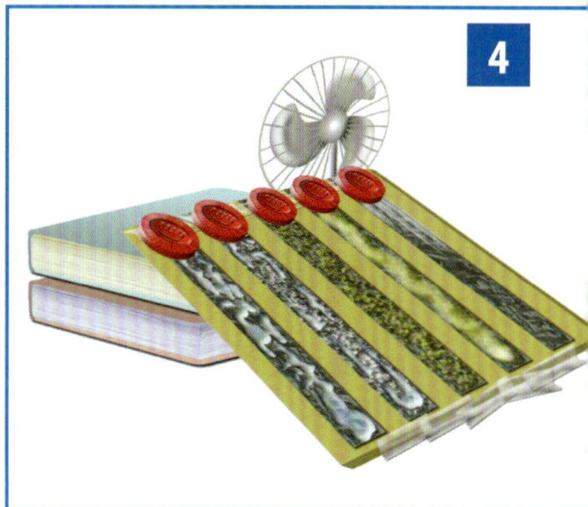

4

5

Glossary

acceleration—a change in speed

aerodynamics—the study of movement of air

bindings—equipment that fastens your feet to a board

center of mass—the point at which an object is balanced

collision—crash

cyclist—person who rides a bicycle

force—a push or pull that makes things move

friction—force that acts on surfaces in contact and slows them down

gravity—force that attracts things to each other

mass—amount of matter in an object

motion—a change in position

physics—the science of force and motion

pressure—application of force

rotation—the act of turning around a point or axis

traction—the sticking power resulting from friction of two objects

Index

Scientists Then and Now

Robert Goddard
(1882–1945)

Robert Goddard wanted to explore space. So, he built rockets! Goddard used Newton's laws to help him. He believed that a rocket could travel all the way to the moon. Goddard was the first to launch a liquid-fueled rocket. In 1926 he tested it. It went about 12 meters (40 feet) high at about 97 kilometers (60 miles) per hour. Goddard did not live to see people travel in space, but his ideas and rockets helped pave the way.

Steven Chu
(1948–)

As a child, Steven Chu liked to build things. He started out building model airplanes and ships. Then he saved his lunch money so that he could build rockets at home! In high school, he built a machine that measured gravity. All these childhood experiments would later help him win a Nobel Prize in physics. He also became the Secretary of Energy for President Barack Obama.

Image Credits

Cover Suzanne Tucker/Shutterstock; p.1 Suzanne Tucker/Shutterstock; p.4 Mana Photo/Shutterstock; p.4 (bottom) Ronen/Shutterstock; p.4 (center) Eric Limon/Shutterstock; p.5 (top) Andrey Khrolenok/Shutterstock; p.6 (left) Tim Bradley; p.6 (left middle) The Granger Collection, New York; p.6 (right middle) The Granger Collection, New York; p.6 (right) The Granger Collection, New York; p.7 (top) PictureArts/Newscom; p.7 (left) ypkim/Shutterstock; p.7 (left middle) Reinhold Foeger/Shutterstock; p.7 (right middle) hamurishi/Shutterstock; p.7 (right) MCT/Newscom; p.8-9 R. Gino Santa Maria/Shutterstock; p.8-9 (bottom) Rob Byron/Shutterstock; p.8 (bottom) The Granger Collection, New York; p.10-11 David G. McIntyre/Newscom; p.11 Mike Powell/Corbis; p.12 Stan Liu/Newscom; p.12-13 KRT/Newscom; p.13 Ben Mitchell/Getty; p.14 James Hudson/Alamy; p.14-15 SueC/Shutterstock; p.15 Alexander Kalina/Shutterstock; p.16 Daniel Gustavsson/Shutterstock; p.17-18 Sebastien Burel/Shutterstock; p.17 ZUMA Press; p.18-19 Steve Robertson/AFP/Getty Images; p. 19 (top) Cheryl Casey/Shutterstock; p.19 (bottom) James Steidl/Shutterstock; p.20 Ben Heys/Shutterstock; p.21 Ipatov/Shutterstock; p.21 (top) Brunswick; p.22 Galina Barskaya/Shutterstock; p.23 Evok20/Shutterstock; p.24 Friedemann Vogel/Bongarts/Getty Images; p.24-25 Sergei Bachlakov/Shutterstock; p.26 (left) Tobias Hase/dpa/Corbis; p.26 (middle) AFP PHOTO/Indranil MUKHERJEE/Newscom; p.26 (right) Jeff Greenberg/Alamy; p.26 (bottom) Jeff Grĕenberg/Alamy; p.27 greenwales/Alamy; p.29 Nicolle Rager Fuller; p.32 (left) NASA p.32 (right) Roy Kaltschmidt/Lawrence Berkeley National Labratory